Instagram Income

How Solo Entrepreneurs and Small Companies Can Make Money on IG

Chris Oberg

Contents

Introduction

We solo entrepreneurs and small business owners usually have one thing in common. We are always looking for ways to make more money, and the faster, the better! Therefore, our eyes are always open to new tactics and strategies for finding new leads and customers. As it happens, many of us turn to social media, particularly Instagram (IG), to market ourselves and our businesses.

As valuable as IG has the potential of being, IG is a tricky monster. If we are not careful, it eats up all our time and energy and spits us out with anxiety, brain fog, and a weird feeling of "gaaah...what am I doing wrong on IG?!"

I know, I've been there.

For me, IG was a frustrating time sink until a few months ago. When I first started marketing my business on IG, I did what most solo entrepreneurs do. I spent a ton of time on the platform, commenting on other posts, chasing more followers (because more is better right?), and" creating content." But, even if the numbers of followers slowly grew and my followers slowly started to engage more and more, something was missing. The missing part is obvious now, but

I couldn't see it back then. The missing piece was that I didn't have a clear picture of where in my business my IG account lived, so I didn't have a clear strategy of how to monetize my IG account.

It took me a year and a half into my IG journey before I realized I had to view my IG account as an **INCOME STREAM** and not a "marketing channel." That slight mindset shift made a huge difference in my IG strategy. If you are serious about making money on IG, I highly suggest you start viewing IG as a potential income stream.

Why Should You Listen to Me when it comes to making money on IG?

I'm going to be very honest with you. I'm a regular Swedish guy living in Sweden. Swedish is my native language (I'm doing my best to hide my broken English). I coach solo entrepreneurs on building profitable self-publishing businesses on Amazon. I have had my IG account a while (check out my profile @inkomstmedbocker), and I have 900+ followers when I write this. 900 is not many followers, I'm aware of that, but you know what? You don't need a ton of followers to make money on IG, and I'm proof of that. Since I started to view my IG account as an income stream instead of a marketing channel a few months ago, I've since earned thousands of dollars and got hundreds of email subscribers from IG, proving you don't need a huge following to make money on IG.

I have no formal business background, but I've taken several great online business programs and courses (shout out to Ramit Sethi). Before starting my business journey, I dedicated a ton of time to online poker. Poker and business/entrepreneurship have a lot in common. Becoming successful in poker is all about seeing the world from other people's perspectives and making calculated strategic decisions based on the available information at hand. Combine that with the core of entrepreneurship (solving problems for a profit), and you have my background. In poker, like in business, good intentions are always lovely. But what matters is getting results. For me, results mean **making money**, which is what this book is all about.

What You'll Learn in This Book

Through these pages, I'm going show you strategies for using Instagram to get real paying customers. Then, we'll take a deep look into seeing how you can use IG to attract the right followers and turn them into paying customers.

In the opening chapter, we'll discuss Instagram's business model and how you can leverage it to your advantage. Then, we'll dive into some strategies for figuring out the purpose of your IG account and how you find a way to monetize your IG account. I'll also show you how to craft your strategy so that Instagram benefits from what you are doing.

The second chapter is all about figuring out your followers' heroes' journeys and finding a solution to their problems in a unique, engaging way. People are bombarded with thousands of images every day, so you must learn to connect with your followers.

The third chapter examines how everything you do on IG can be viewed as a product. We will also kill the expression "content creating" and start running your first money-making experiments. I'll show you some of my successful (and not so successful) IG experiments.

The fourth chapter is all about money and how to monetize your account, including different ways of selling products, different IG sales funnels, selling in DM, and much more.

Let's get started!

Chapter one: Figure out how you are going to make money on IG

I firmly believe that your money-making IG strategy should be aligned with IG's business model. If IG themselves likes what you are doing, your account will get more organic exposure, and IG will automatically push your IG account to more people. Here's how to accomplish that.

Instagram's Business Model

Why are people scrolling on IG? Simply put, they WANT to be distracted. They're looking for something that hooks their attention. The people scrolling on IG are the product of which IG is making money. IG is designed to make people spend as much time as possible on there. And for you to make money on IG, you need to create something that hooks the IG users' attention and makes them want to spend more time on IG. Therefore, your posts, videos, and all your content must be aligned with IG's business model.

Like most social media platforms, IG monetizes its platform by keeping people on there for as long as possible. Every little thing on IG, from the colors to the beeping sounds, is designed to trick people into spending more time on there. It's scary when you think about it, but that's the reality. For example, it's no coincidence that the IG feed is somewhat randomized, similar to a slot machine. You never know when you log in on IG. Will you hit the jackpot and find something that hooks your attention or not? Your IG feed is entirely different from mine because IG keeps serving content that interests and engages you, and it keeps serving me content that interests me. That way, we all end up happy.

While IG looks innocent from the outside with its clean interface and beautiful images, in reality, everything is carefully engineered with one goal in mind: monetize our attention. I like to use the analogy that IG is like a slot machine. In the same way, a slot machine keeps gamblers engaged and entertained, IG keeps us all entertained and distracted to make sure we spend as much of our free time on there as possible. And when you do, you are making money for IG. Once that happens, IG will throw you other stuff to grab your attention so that they can make even more money off you.

Knowing how IG is making money can help in many ways when you start crafting your money-making IG strategy. First, given how IG works, if your strategy aligns with IG's business model, you will increase the chances of IG picking up your account and recommending it to more people. Secondly, knowing that IG is like a slot machine that tries to monetize your attention can help to put clear boundaries around how you use IG. For example, the purpose of having an IG account is not to casually spend your valuable time and energy on IG. Instead, the goal is to use IG to make money for you and your business and do so while IG leaves a minimal footprint on your time and mental energy.

Your Business Model

Take a step back and look at your business from above. Look at all the ways people come to know about you, how they find your homepage, how they see your physical store if you have one, and how customers and clients refer you to their friends and family. Think about all the different paths these people take, from not knowing about you to doing business with you. Do you see all the different ways? Good. Now, think about where IG has a clear place in that mix.

In the early stages of my 1:1 coaching business, I didn't think too much about IG, focusing my attention and efforts on Facebook group posting and Google SEO (search engine optimization) instead. As a result, I thought that it was hard to sell on IG. The mistake I made was a classic one. I treated IG the same way I treated Google SEO. SEO lives at the top of the business funnel for most businesses, bringing in users looking for answers to questions or simple information about something.

On the other hand, IG is different and lives further down in the business funnel. Making money on IG comes down to grabbing attention and building engagement with one's followers. And when I talk about engagement, I don't mean a "like" on a post. Engagement for me means either commenting on or sharing my post, sending me a DM, or visiting my website.

When I shifted towards focusing on getting attention and engagement instead of "providing information," I quickly started to see the potential of IG. IG then helped me accomplish two things in my 1:1 coaching business. First, and most importantly, I was able to skyrocket the number of sales calls I booked from doing an attention/engagement stories-post --> DM conversation --> sales call. And secondly, I've got hundreds of email subscribers by pointing the URL in my profile to my lead magnet. For me, pretty much everything I do on IG either points people to contact me in DM or visit my website (with the end goal of them subscribing to my mailing list). That's how I monetize my IG account.

You might have a completely different business model. You might be able to monetize your IG account differently but to get you thinking about what you can do on IG, think about how your business is making money and where in your business IG fits the best. What type of products and services are you selling? Your IG strategy will be different if you run a 1:1 online coaching business as I do or if you own a local bakery and are trying to get more people to buy your cakes.

Having a clear goal for what you want to accomplish (more traffic to your e-commerce store? more email subscribers or sign-ups to your webinar, or booking more sales calls in IG DMs as I do?) will help you tremendously when you craft your money-making IG strategy. But before we talk more about strategy, let's figure out how to get the attention and engagement you first and foremost need to make money on IG.

How to get attention and engagement on IG

If we know that IG monetizes people's attention, we also know that you effectively have to get your followers' attention and engagement to make money on IG. If your followers scroll past your posts without any engagement, you will have difficulty making money on IG. So step one in your strategy should get your followers' attention. If you haven't started your IG account yet, and don't have any followers yet, keep these tips in mind when you do.

One of the main reasons why people use IG daily is curiosity. When we find something that gets us curious and hooks our attention, our brain releases dopamine and serotonin, the "happy hormones," which give us a pleasant feeling. We crave that feeling! The IG slot machine does a fantastic job of delivering a boost of serotonin and dopamine. I'm not a neuroscience expert, but I know a few strategies for getting the right kind of attention and engagement on IG.

Connect, don't convince

It goes without saying, but whenever someone interacts with your IG account, they wish to receive value. Of course, the idea of value varies from one person to another. Still, you can think about your followers, prospects, and previous customers' hopes, fears, and dreams. That's what you want to connect to. What problem are you solving for your followers? What are the benefits they looking for? By connecting with their hopes, fears, and dreams, you are signaling that you understand them, care about them, and they will be more open to listening to what you have to say. In other words, you got their attention! Bingo!

Focusing on connecting instead of convincing stands out as authentic among all internet marketers out there. Think about it: if all you do on IG is try to convince your followers to buy your products, your followers will grow tired of you pretty damn fast. So instead, try one of these tips to connect with your followers.

Make It About Them and meet them where they are

Rather than rambling on about your product, try shifting things towards the issues of your followers. What would their needs be at this moment that caused them to seek out your IG account? What is something that is most important to them right now? Don't make it about you or your product; instead, make it about them. Ask them many questions and listen to what they have to say. You can DM them or do Q&As in stories and listen carefully to what they have to say. If you do that, you will have a well of valuable insight into why your followers are following you, and you can more easily connect with their hope, fears, and dreams.

I'm ALWAYS on the hunt for insight about my followers. In my coaching business, I coach people on making money by self-publishing on Amazon, but the REAL reason people are following me on IG has nothing to do with Amazon. They follow me because they want to learn how to gain more financial freedom in their lives, and that's the story I try to connect to. I could post self-publishing strategies all day long, but that would fall on deaf ears. So instead, I meet them where they are, and I can speak directly to their hope, fears, and dreams.

Asking for insight and what's going on inside your followers' minds opens up all kinds of opportunities. For example, you may have a testimonial from a previous client or a relevant case study. Since you know these people had similar concerns, you can connect more deeply with them.

Show Them You Care about them

If you wish to inspire your followers to do business with you, you need to put less of an emphasis on what you are selling and instead talk about the benefits of using your product or service. How will your product or service help them? Can you prove that you have already helped people like them before? Do you understand all of the problems that they are going through? Rather than talking about all your product's features, talk about its benefits and what it can do for them. Show that what you care about is solving their problem.

One of my entrepreneurial friends, Marie is doing this better than anyone I know. She has so much insight about her followers (mostly 25-55-year-old women looking to find their life's task). She can pretty much read her follower's minds, and the engagement she gets on her posts is insane! She speaks right to her followers' hearts and connects deeply. For example, when she launched her group coaching program, she made $8,000 from 600 followers in TWO DAYS! How cool isn't that? I'll share how she did it later in this book.

The purpose of your IG account

Start with your business model in mind, and think about what you want to accomplish with your IG account. Then work backward. If your goal is to bring more customers to your e-commerce store, your reason for having an IG account is to drive traffic, and everything you will do on IG must somehow support that goal. I'll show you a detailed example of how I use IG to drive traffic later in this book. On the other hand, if you are a physical therapist and are using IG to get new leads, your best strategy might be to personally contact all your existing and new followers, one by one, to build a relationship and connect with them.

Regardless of what you want to accomplish, think about how IG can benefit from what you are doing. Nobody knows how the IG algorithm works. You don't have to worry about that either as long as you focus on connecting with your followers, getting attention and engagement, and knowing how everything you post on IG fits within your business model.

Chapter two: Be the Guide on your followers heroes journey

One of the people I follow in the personal brand space is Mike Kim. Mike has a podcast, and he recently launched his instant bestselling book *You Are The Brand*. In episode #301 of Mike's podcast, he brought up an interesting idea that had been on my mind for years: that most of the so-called "influencers" basically have very little or sometimes *nothing* valuable to say. I usually call this the "influencer trap". Many people aspire to be "influencers," but they come at it from I-I-I point of view and think that simply sharing whatever message *they* feel like (like what they had for lunch) will gain them popularity and make them rich and famous. I think that's a big mistake many people make when they set out to make money on IG. I like Mikes's take on this because he divided "influence" into three categories. These three categories are experts, influencers, and thought leaders.

Experts have tons of knowledge and cutting-edge expertise, but almost nobody knows about them, and very few people follow them. Think about a math professor, for example.

Influencers, on the other hand (often), have little or no expert knowledge about a particular subject, but many people (somehow) follow them.

The combination of both of them, with expert knowledge and many followers, is what Mike calls "thought leaders." Think about someone like Tony Robins in the personal development space.

If we take Mike's concept of "thought leaders," and instead of just applying it to personal brand business, we apply it to small companies as well, what we end up with is something we can call a "Guide."

Be the Guide

If there's something we humans love, it's a good old hero's journey, especially if we are the hero. With that journey in mind, you know the story where the hero overcomes all kinds of obstacles only to crash again, feel overwhelmed, dust their shoulders off, and keep going to reach his or her full potential. That's how you need to view your IG followers. They are heroes on their journey. So, what does that make you? You are the Guide, or rather, your company sells the guiding principles, the solution, the equipment, and the training. Your company is the compass the heroes will follow. They'll look to you for inspiration, motivation, and the resources to keep going even on the darkest of nights. They'll look to your IG posts for the voice of reassurance.

Generally speaking, people's main life challenges are lack of money, health, or unsuccessful relationships. People are likely following you to solve a problem in one of these areas. Your business can be a guide to those looking for financial freedom, success, or better health. You can provide them with the tools they need to get there and show them how to use these tools effectively by being their Guide on IG.

Once you gather a following that begins to trust you and see you as the Guide, that's when your IG income potential will start to blossom. It is tough to monetize IG, even if you have plenty of followers, if you don't solve real problems for real people. Positioning yourself as the Guide and having real influence gives you much more leverage to sell your products on IG, and the beautiful benefit of this approach is that you don't need tons of followers to make money on IG. In my opinion, this approach allows you to monetize your IG account from day one.

Being the Guide and having real influence is understanding the challenges your followers' experience, then providing a solution uniquely and interestingly. By doing so, your IG account will become like a magnet that draws people in, and you can do this in all niches.

Becoming the Guide is a relatively easy, but not a simple, endeavor. The hard part is finding what your market wants to read, seeing what they're interested in, and creating solutions to their problems.

Compare the Guide approach to the standard influencer approach. Guides don't call themselves "influencers." They don't feel the need to label themselves as influencers. They're too busy doing exciting stuff and sharing their ideas with their followers. However, many tend to label themselves as "influencers" without having any real influence. These people are called influencers, not because of their advice or the content they produce but because they have many followers. Self-proclaimed influencers are full of themselves, share shallow ideas, and force useless content down our throats, and by the way, most of them are struggling to make money on IG.

To become the Guide, you need to be an interesting individual with interesting things to share, and you need to be authentic in your way. Naturally, that is easier said than done, but it offers an alternative to the term "influencer" many of us are getting tired of.

In today's marketing world, there's much talk about "content creation." But is that the only thing that matters to make money on IG? I don't think so. What is often missing is being interesting and connecting to your followers. Many so-called "content creators" settle for putting out tons of shallow content, which builds a nice library of content, sure, but that's not what IG is about. A library of the content does not equal money in the bank.

Being interesting, authentic, and focusing on your money-making IG strategy (getting attention, engagement, and leading people where you want them to go), that's what is going to earn you money.

As previously touched upon, when you approach IG with a connecting mentality, you need to ask your followers the right questions to get the proper insight. And with the right insight, you use these as building blocks for all your content. That way, you can soon read your followers' minds like my friend Marie.

Each of your followers has different hopes, fears, and dreams and has their hero's journey. To connect with them, you must ask them questions, even if it is scary at first. You can ask them questions in many ways; preferably, I try to get my followers on a video call, but DM works fine too.

Figure out your followers' real pain points

I've borrowed this three-step structure from Ramit Sethi. Every time I get the chance to chat with one of my followers and feel like they can open up, I rely on this structure in my hunt for insights.

1. Get them to open Up

When you ask a question to a follower, you need to do it in a manner that will get them to open up to you. For example, let's say that your question has many facts wrapped into it. As a result, instead of being a question like it is supposed to be, it ends up being a statement where you are looking for agreement or feedback. But unfortunately, this doesn't pave the way for the follower to open up to you.

To get your follower to open up, you might want to ask them short questions asked in a simple form. Focus on whys and hows and give them incentives to open up to you. "Can you explain that, please," or "could you offer some examples" are a great way to get things started.

Connecting with your followers is a two-way street. Not only do you need to connect with them, but they need to connect with you as well. This is the only way that they will be able to open up to you.

2. **Discover Their Needs**

Every question that you ask must have a purpose – and in this case, it should be to find out their needs. If you managed to get the follower to open up in the first stage, you need to get them to spill out the right info. Many questions may help you out for that purpose, but here are just some of them that you can use:

- What made you interested in following this account? [they might answer something like, "I want to learn more about how to get in shape"]
- What is the main thing that is preventing you from achieving [insert the outcome they want]
- What are your short-term goals? What about the long-term ones?
- Are there any ways for me/us to better meet your needs?
- What do you consider to be your priorities right now?

The questions may change depending on your niche, the service you are providing, and the follower you are dealing with. Sometimes, the best way could be to jump the gun right away with the question, "what are your current needs?" and when they answer, say, "Great, I have a product that will help you accomplish that. Would you be willing to book a 30-min sales call to see if it's a good fit?"

Also, you must be aware that you'll have to ask many follow-up questions. Sometimes, even the customer may not know what their need is – so, you'll have to tap into their mind to find out.

3.   Be Careful with Emotional Landmines

How often have you asked a question to a prospect, client, or follower only to see everything eventually blow up in your direction? I remember one particular time when that happened to me. This one lady reached out to me, asked a few questions, and asked if we could book a 30-min consultation call. My first thought was, "yes! She wants to buy my program! I better get on that call!". We booked the call three days later, but that didn't stop her from emailing me long emails days before the call. Those were very emotional emails, including her desires, her broken dreams, and how society didn't believe in her.

We got on the call three days later. My initial plan was obviously to sell my coaching program, but that call somehow turned into a 1,5hr therapy session. When I asked her why she reached out to me, she told me her entire back story. And when we talked about price, it became obvious to me that she had no buying intent whatsoever. I was completely drained after that call, but the lesson was a good one: if you sense that you have stepped on the wrong emotional landmine, get the hell out of there asap!

However, if you step on the right emotional landmine, you might trigger an even stronger connection with your follower by using their emotions to your advantage.

Think about the many times you blurted out your needs just because you got emotional about something. It's in our nature – and you can be sure this will happen to your followers as well. This is why it's wise to ask questions that evoke emotions – for example, desire, arousal, and so on.

Strategies for creating connecting content

Everything suddenly becomes interesting when you set out to help your followers on their journey by showcasing empathy and staying true to yourself. Everything they say to you can be used to create posts that connect with them. With the two simple questions, "Which hero's journey am I helping with?" and "How am I helping?" you can find ideas everywhere.

I like to read, and books contain valuable ideas. When I read, I always look for small concepts, quotes, or something that feels authentic and how that can relate to my followers. That said, you can also draw ideas from movies, TV shows, artwork, or anywhere else. If you can figure out how to connect your content to these bigger sources, you can easily inspire people and guide them on their own hero's journey.

Developing a form of unique taste

What distinguishes the "shallow" content from the transformative and follow-worthy content you're going to post is your taste and how you blend your ideas with taste. Developing a form of unique taste and how you solve your followers' hero's journey is what will help to make you interesting. Invariably, that taste can only come from developing a solid ground and knowledge about your followers and everything related to them. Perhaps you have a taste for history, so you include in a lot of historical anecdotes, or you have a taste for a particular cuisine, so you blend your content with that, or you have a strong taste for a certain type of fashion, and you develop something around that.

This is why the two-pronged approach of understanding your audience (what's important to them, what hero's journey they're on, what problems you solve for them) and developing your taste is so important. It helps you connect with your audience in a way they'll find interesting and also helps you find ideas about what could be interesting to them.

Sharing what you know also means sharing your mistakes or failures so that others can learn from them and save themselves the time, effort, and financial resources you've invested in learning those lessons. You can share both your own and others' personal stories, provide tips on how to solve problems, solutions to problems you've solved for your audience in the past, and more. The most important thing about sharing what you know is that, by doing so, you develop your taste when it comes to the things that interest your followers. Think of it as your emotional fingerprint. The only way to develop your emotional fingerprint is by keeping an eye on what interests your followers and staying in touch with them.

Lastly, but importantly, because Instagram is a platform where people discover new content, you can afford to experiment with different types of content. For instance, you can upload photos of the things you love, links to articles or interviews with influencers in your industry, fun facts about your line of work, and anything related to your niche or interests. Bottom line, it doesn't matter what type of content you upload as long as it's interesting and relevant to your target audience.

Exercise: brainstorm ten different posts

It's time to package everything we have covered so far and start experimenting on IG. The only way to make money on IG is to get practical, which means posting, testing, and seeking honest feedback from your followers. Think about how you can position yourself as the hero on your followers' journey and brainstorm a few different ideas you can turn into IG posts.

Chapter three: Running Your Money Making Experiments

IG offers the perfect environment for running money-making experiments. You can make a post in under 30 minutes and almost instantly see if you hit your target or not. If a particular type of post catches your followers' attention and yields the results you're after, do more of that! And if a specific kind of post flops, great! You view that as a valuable experiment and try the next thing. Your strategy should be a bit loose and fluid, constantly experimenting with new things to crack the winning formula of what resonates with your followers. In this chapter, I will show you how to run these experiments at rapid speed, viewing everything you post on IG as a *product*.

If you are new to IG with zero followers

If you are just getting started on IG and have zero or very few followers, you are in for a treat! It seems like the IG algorithm is pushing and boosting new accounts to (much) more organic exposure compared to older accounts. It makes sense that IG does that. IG wants you (the user) to get as many followers as fast as possible because then you will feel like many people are hyped about what you are doing, which will make you spend more time on IG (so IG can monetize your attention). More than that, IG wants to keep recommending new accounts in their "discovery feed" for users to explore.

When you are new to IG, I just want you to be careful. The purpose of having an IG account is to make money and contribute to your business's bottom line. It's not about chasing random followers or getting hyped about how many "likes" you get.

If you have an existing following on IG

Regardless of whether you have a small or large IG following, and regardless of your previous IG strategies, be ready to lose some of your followers as soon as you start these money-making experiments. Losing followers hurts, but it's a good thing. Followers who are not interested in what you offer are dead weight, and you want to segment your existing followers as soon as possible to remove that weight. That being said, you will eventually get more new followers, but older accounts are a bit tricky to "wake up" and require more work before the algorithm picks them up and starts "boosting" them like new accounts. Therefore, you might lose more followers than you gain when beginning with this new approach.

See All Your IG Posts as Products

Eli Schwart's book Product Led SEO truly opened my eyes to SEO. In that book, Eli talks about why most SEO strategies are flawed (they tend to only focus on Google rankings) and why every SEO effort should be viewed as being a *product*.

He means that every piece of SEO content should be carefully designed to attract the customers' desires and lead them somewhere with the end goal of turning them into customers. I love that concept. Just think about it... How many times haven't you heard that SEO is all about rankings? Sure, rankings may be important but ranking high on Google isn't worth anything unless the traffic contributes to the bottom line.

When I read Eli's book, I got an epiphany moment when I understood that the same concept could be applied to IG! I blew my mind when I realized that everything I do on IG could be viewed as a PRODUCT. Everything you post on IG, whether they're feed-posts, stories, or videos, have a few ingredients. You have an image or video file, written text, and most important of all, the underlying "problem" (or hero's journey) your content (post, story, video) is supporting. When you package all those ingredients, you have a product. A feed-post is a type of product. A stories-post is a product. A 20-sec reel is a product. Everything your followers consume from you can be viewed as a product.
When your followers are using your product (namely, consuming your content), the product guides your followers throughout their journey so that they'll want to use more of your products. Posting on IG then becomes a kind of chain where every post is a small product.

The purpose of a product is to make money

The purpose of putting out a product (posting on IG) should be to make money. However, it doesn't mean all your posts have to be sales posts, but rather that all your posts should fit within your business funnel. Now, here's the big difference between this approach and the "content creation" approach. When a "content creator" posts something, more often than not, it does not sync with the overall business funnel and therefore does not contribute to the business bottom line.

Two of my money-making experiments

When you start thinking about which product to create, spend a few minutes planning out what you want to accomplish with the product you have in mind. If you are doing a feed-post, what are you hoping to accomplish? When I do a feed-post, I want people to comment, and I want to take the conversation to DM and work my magic there. Here's an example of how I did that with a simple feed video experiment.

Look at this video here:

The quality is pretty bad, the lighting is bad, and I'm looking a bit tired too. And it only got 225 views and five comments. What a failure! Or?

No.

What's not showing here is how this video made me $400.

Take a look at those comments below the video.

That's real engagement. She is interested in what I'm saying. When you get real engagement in comments like this, consider that green light to move the conversation to DM.

We chatted in DM, and I did my best to connect with her in my hunt for more insights into her desires.

From DM, we took the conversation to email and onto Zoom, and she signed up for one of my coaching programs.

That's a long funnel, I know. It's many steps from the comments to the sale, but that's what a simple video experiment can result in, even if I look like a "failure" from the outside.

Lesson learned from this test:
Don't overthink your experiments. Even an "ugly" video with 225 views can make money on IG... as long as it fits within your business funnel!

I love selling in IG stories. For me, stories are the most powerful sales tool on IG. IG recently added the ability for all of us to include URL links in our stories, which is super powerful. My default strategy for selling in IG stories is to have 3-5 slides, divided into three categories. The first category is aimed at getting attention and connection, the second is to build some context, and the third is to direct/link my followers to a website or encourage them to take some kind of action.

Here's a story-funnel I spent 2 hours doing and got zero engagement (this story was originally posted in Swedish):

Can you see why this test didn't work?

Looking at this eight-slide funnel now, It's clear to me that this funnel is way too long and probably a bit too boring as well. I should have shortened it, changed the fonts and images, and talked about the benefits of my coaching programs much more. But hey, I didn't, and that's fine. I simply wrote that off as a valuable experiment and kept my head high.

Are you ready to start experimenting with your products?

Create Your Product

It's time to package everything we have talked about so far and create your product (aka, doing your posts). Take everything into account and think about how you are the guide, think about your followers' hero's journey, their underlying questions, include your unique taste, take the plunge, and create your product. Most IG pros advocate for "content categories" or "content buckets," which means a few broad categories you constantly produce products (create content) around. For a wellness coach, that might be one around exercising, one around dieting, and one around recovering and resting. You can go as broad or narrow as you wish. Typically, I don't overthink the content buckets that much, yet it's a strategy to keep in mind to make sure you connect with all types of people within your niche.

For instance, let's say you decide to run an experiment with a two-slide feed post. For doing that, you need an image, and you need to write some copy. So here's how to get it right:

Start your Canva account

Countless tools can help facilitate and perfect your IG game. For example, I create my posts in Canva. Canva is an online graphic design tool that makes photo editing a breeze. It has a massive database of free images, fonts, and layouts for you to use to create beautiful, eye-catching posts. Set up a Canva account (canva.com) and look around at their layouts.

Picking the right image

Instagram is a highly visible platform, meaning that the image is a big part of your product. The general rule is to design something that "breaks through the noise", while knowing that the goal of your product is to connect with your followers on their journey. In other words, you don't want to stand out for the wrong reasons but rather fit in within the context of the problem you're trying to solve. You are not concerned about standing out for the sake of standing out since that will never lead to more sales. Instead, you want your images to be like a magnet that your followers will enjoy.

I'm not a very talented visual artist, and my design skills are limited. My strategy has always been to let my copywriting skills do more of the selling. That said, if your image sucks, it's going to be hard to get the attention you need to make money. I recommend starting with something extremely basic, like a white background or a simple image. That's enough in the testing phase. The purpose is not to get it perfect; the purpose is to get started.

For the sake of this experiment, let's pretend you are an online yoga instructor, and your purpose for using IG is to get more leads and signups to your online course. You have tried IG before, but it didn't really "click, " and you are now giving it a new shoot. Your first step should be to choose an image that matches your followers' hero's journey. For example, their hero's journey could be "living a stress-free life," so you pick an image that's signals yoga and calmness, like this one:

Let's keep that image and move on to what you write in your image and your caption.

Copywriting for IG

Copywriting is the most undervalued skill in marketing. I don't know why, maybe because it's sexier to talk about ad spend and the hottest hashtags of the day? But let's be real here, getting good at copywriting can dramatically improve how much money you make on IG. Everything you write on IG is copywriting in one form or another—every single word. The text you include in your images is copywriting. The text you write in your caption is copywriting. Everything you write is copywriting.

The copywriting formula AIDA

There are many different formulas for writing copy, and there are many different forms of copy. I highly recommend you take the time to learn the different types of copy you write in your business. Still, as a starting point for writing good enough IG posts, I recommend AIDA's classic copywriting formula. AIDA stands for attention, interest, desire, and action.

Attention

Step number one is always to get people's attention. If you can't get their attention, it will be hard to accomplish anything. How do you get someone's attention on IG? It's not easy these days, but there are a few things you can do. First of all, you need to write directly to your target market. The words you use must be tailored to your target market. Making money on IG is not about getting everyone's attention and "breaking through the noise," as discussed earlier. It's getting the right people's attention. That's all that matters. When you design your images, don't think about what you think "looks good." Think instead about your target market. The same goes for headlines. Don't write "catchy" headlines for the sake of being catchy. Write headlines that resonate with your market!

Interest/Desire

When you have got your target market's attention, now what? Now it's time to start digging deeper, getting them to listen to what you have to say. This is the trickiest part. If you got their attention but didn't follow up with something interesting, they will most likely continue scrolling and never return.

Let's say you write an attention-grabbing image text and get your ideal customer to stop their scroll. What you need to do now is to build up interest by sharing something they care about. You can do that by telling a story that resonates with them or talking about anything related to their hopes, fears, and dreams. The trick here is always to think, "what's in it for them? What's in it for them?" It's not about you at this stage; it's about them. It's about their interest, not yours.

When you nail the interest/desire part of your copy, your audience wants MORE. The copy you wrote has aroused them, got their blood pumping, and the dopamine flowing in their bodies. They want more, and they want it NOW.

Do you see how that works? You are not forcing them on anything at this point; you have grabbed their attention and built up their interest. You are almost there; all you need now is not to screw up the action part.

Action

You have probably heard of the term CTA before, which stands for *call to action*. CTAs are super important in copywriting. CTAs are what make people buy your stuff, sign up for your email list, reach out to you, like your posts (not that important, but it's still an action), and tell their friends about how awesome you are.

A CTA is a prompt, statement, or question at the end of your copy that works like an invisible hand that gets people to act on whatever you want them to act upon.

Here's the one thing that most people miss with a good CTA: you can never force someone to do something. An act must come from within; otherwise, it's manipulation. If you have done your job by getting their attention and making them interested in what you have to say, the CTA doesn't need to be written in bold letters with tons of exclamation marks. All you need to do is lead them wherever you want them to go.

Many people talk about CTA as if it's all that matters, but they are wrong. A CTA itself can rarely do all the heavy lifting. As the business owner, you must get your prospects' attention, take them on a journey in your interest/desire phase, and leave them with the decision to act on your CTA. If you have done your job right, they will almost always act on the CTA. The key here (again) is to be authentic and know your audience, focusing on them and always asking yourself, "what's in it for them."

Copy in the image

For me, including some written text in my images works better than not doing it, but I've heard that many people report the opposite. Selfies are the best, they say. Test what works best for you, but if you decide to include some text in your images, here's how I would do it.

If you decide to do a one slide feed post

Consider the written text in your image as a "headline." Writing good headlines can be tricky and require some training. A few tips on writing a good headline:

- Include digits instead of words, like "5" instead of "five."
- Be extremely specific.
- Create urgency and frame it as a "secret" or an "idea"

If we go back to the yoga example above and want to make a product about the five benefits of yoga, we could write a headline that says "Five Benefits of doing Yoga." That's not bad, but it's not particularly good either. On the other hand, if we change that headline to "5 secret benefits of doing yoga," I'm sure more people would stop their scroll and read our post.

If you have two or more images

A popular trend is to include all text in the images and post several images in one post like a carousel. This works so well because it's much easier to read for the user than reading a long caption. Remember to follow the AIDA formula and learn from my eight-slide story-funnel above if you decide to do that. Another benefit of including more than one image in your post is that IG gives every post a second chance and will use the second image as the "front image" when they show the post the second time.

Writing captions

The caption is the text that's below the image. The first part of the caption, the text visible before the "read more" is your attention part. The "read more" button is there because IG knows that most people are not reading the caption.

I think the best type of captions is like an image extension, and it's clear that the image and the caption work together. I've played around with different types of caption openers and what works best for me speaks directly to my followers. I try to avoid "I," "my," and other self-centric openers when I write captions. To get the right tone and voice in my captions, I always do the images first and write caption afterward, and I look at the image when I write the caption. That way, the image and the caption have the same vibe.

Stories copy

Your followers have no idea what you have posted in stories before they open up your stories. Therefore, your stories' open rate is critical to get the most out of your stories. I recommend mixing things up in stories to make your followers curious about what you have posted. If you are doing 99% sales stories, your followers will quickly grow tired of you and stop opening your stories. I use stories to sell, drive traffic, build engagement, entertain, inform, and do all kinds of things! Since you can post several stories slides in a row, similar to a "sales funnel," you can take your followers on a little stories journey.

If you decide to try a stories funnel with the end goal of generating traffic back to your website, a thing I've noticed is including the CTA two times to increase the chance of your followers acting on it.

Look at this funnel:

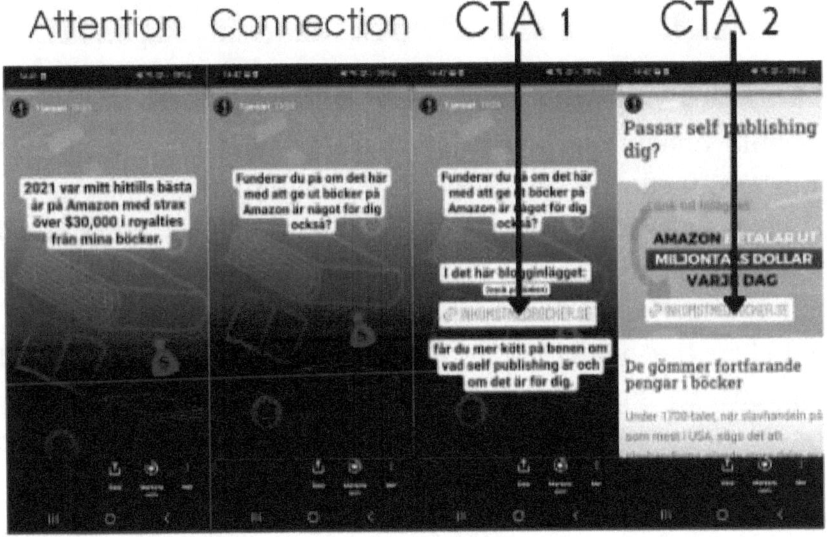

Result in traffic:

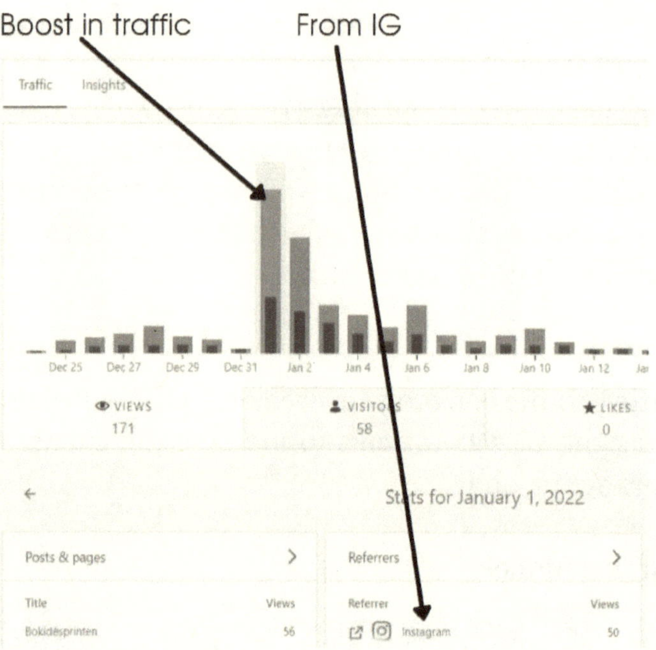

Keep the winners and seek actual proof

I would encourage you to start experimenting and putting your products out there as soon as possible. There is no better way to make money on IG than doing the work. That being said, The market will tell you if your post resonated or not. If you hear nothing, that's the market telling you loud and clear that your product (posts) wasn't a good fit. If that happens, try something new! On the other hand, if you get a ton of responses, likes, DMs, that's the market telling you your posts did resonate, and I would recommend you to do all you can to lead those people closer to a sale by setting up sales calls, sending links to your products or inviting them to your store. Spending time following up and speaking directly to your followers will multiply your chances of making money on IG.

When you find a product combination that's working, double down on that. And remember, working is more than just "likes." The ultimate proof of a product's success is if you get IG to make money, so if you manage to get IG to generate revenue, well done! You've cracked the code.

How to grow your IG audience

A common topic of conversation about making money on IG is how to grow your IG following best. However, as you know, the number of followers does not correlate with how much money a specific person is making on IG. With that said, you still need followers to make money on IG, and you need some strategy for keeping your account growing at a steady pace.

The top 50 strategy

In Russell Brunson's book *Traffic Secrets*, Brunson talks about a strategy he has successfully used to grow his podcast, email list, and social channels. He calls it the top 100 strategy. The basic idea of that strategy is to build relationships with the top 100 accounts within your niche. All the followers you want are probably already following one of the top 100 accounts within your niche. So when you build a relationship with the top 100 accounts, it becomes like a bridge between you and the followers you are after.

I think the top 100 strategy is a perfect example of an honest, authentic strategy to grow your account, but following 100 large IG accounts in your niche may seem a bit much, so I have moderated Russell's strategy to the top 50 strategy.

How the top 50 strategy works in practice:

Start following 50 large accounts in your niche and gradually build a relationship with those accounts by liking their photos, commenting on relevant posts, writing with them in DM, etc. For this strategy to work, you need to be genuinely interested in knowing them. You do not want them to get the feeling that you are writing to them just because you want something in return. As soon as you have a somewhat established relationship with one or more of the larger accounts, start sharing their posts in your stories. Then it is only a matter of time before they share one of your posts or stick one of your comments in their comment field. Once that happens, you will see a flood of new followers starting to follow you.

I've used the top 50 strategy to get more followers, and it works great. Sweden is a relatively small country, so my 900+ followers may not look so impressive, but it is easier said than done to grow an account to the magic 10k limit in Sweden.

Use IG's new features

One way to increase the spread of your posts and thus increase the chances of getting new followers is to use IG's latest features. As I write this, IG reels are the latest feature that seems to provide the best spread, but IG is constantly updating and changing the platform, so it may be that reels have been removed when you are reading this. So, ask yourself which is the newest feature on IG right now and use it as much as you possibly can.

Algorithm pushes

We all love tactics and strategies for getting more followers, but the best (and most difficult) way to grow on IG is to get IG to pick up your account and start recommending it on its own. If you scroll in your feed, you will see a section called "suggestions for you." If you click around in stories, you will see the same section there. These are areas that IG itself uses to promote accounts. IG could very well have used this space for ads instead, but they want you as a user to find new accounts to follow so that you get the best experience out of using IG. In addition, IG keeps a close eye on what preferences we have, what pictures we like, and what posts we read. In this way, IG can tailor individual account recommendations to all of us.

For IG to pick up your account, IG needs to know what type of account you have. Otherwise, they can never recommend your account to the right user. I who follow many business accounts usually get suggestions to follow other business accounts. I never get suggestions on following home decorating accounts or cooking accounts. IG knows what kind of posts I like and does its best to make it easy for me to find more similar accounts, so that I spend more time on the platform. Take an extra look at the type of accounts you get as" suggestions for you," which indicates what IG thinks your account is about.

Some common pitfalls make it difficult for IG to know what type of account you have. In the short term, these pitfalls can get you new followers, but it destroys your chances of growing in the long run. The most common of these pitfalls is to jump on the so-called "follower train," which means about 20 accounts begin to follow each other. The problem with this is that as long as not all of these 20 accounts are within the same niche, IG gets confused about your target audience, and IG has a hard time knowing whom to recommend your account to. If you have several followers who in turn follow accounts in training, horse jumping, home decor, but you have a business in cooking, then you have a problem.

Another common pitfall is "giveaways," which means that you give away a prize to everyone who likes one of your posts and chooses to follow you. Unfortunately, if you host giveaways, you will also confuse IG, as lots of people will start following you to be in the draw for a prize.

The timeless strategy for growing your IG account is to always provide awesome products (posts) to your target audience. It is the only thing that will work if you have IG as a source of income.

Hashtags

A user on IG can choose to follow specific hashtags. A hashtag looks like this "#" and is a type of "category" of posts. For example, if someone posts a post with #summer, it will be visible to some followers who have chosen to follow the hashtag #summer.

Sometimes there is much chatter around finding the "best" hashtags, but I think hashtags are a bit overrated. Once you have posted a post, you can look at the post's statistics. For example, you can see how many extra impressions the post got from your hashtags. Usually, it is about 5-10% extra impression from hashtags.

Hashtags give an extra small boost to the spread, which can get you more followers. Still, my recommendation is to make awesome posts and choose relevant hashtags without overthinking them.

Chapter four: Monetize Your IG account

The tricky part about selling on IG is the same as other online selling channels. Your followers must know you are selling something, which means you must talk about your products and services in your posts. Consistency is key here. Simply mentioning it here and there won't magically get your followers to hand you money. In this chapter, we will look at different ways to monetize your IG account.

Marketing rule of 7

There is a "marketing rule of 7" rule in sales and marketing. That rule says a person on average needs to be exposed to a product/service seven times before the person in question buys the product/service. These exposures can be called contact points. A contact point can be to see a product in the IG feed, IG stories, hear about it on a podcast, or have a friend recommend it. The rule of seven applies to the highest degree to everything you sell on IG.

To visualize how the rule of seven works, let's pretend you have 1 000 followers on IG, and all your followers see your offer seven times, making it a total of 7 000 impressions. Now, pretend instead that you have 7 000 followers, and everyone sees your offer one time, which is also 7 000 impressions.

In which scenario do you think you would have sold the most?

If the marketing rule of 7 is true, you would have sold more if the same 1,000 people had seen your offer seven times compared to if 7,000 different people had seen it only once. The reason why is quite simple. Humans are drawn to what we recognize and are often not as attracted to foreign things.

Putting the rule of seven in motion is about increasing the number of contact points between your followers and your offer. Of course, it's easier said than done, but the key here is to keep putting the same offer in front of the same people in different ways.

Talk about your offer in stories

Stories automatically disappear after 24 hours, so you want to make sure people see them. As I've said before, stories are my favorite sales tool on IG. You can use stories to generate leads, drive traffic, draw attention to certain products or even ask your followers specific questions. You can do so much in stories. Only your imagination will be the limit.

The IG stories sales funnel

A simple framework I've used in stories multiple times with great results is the mini sales funnel, typically 3-6 slides and built on top of the AIDA copywriting formula.

The goal of the first slide is to get my followers' attention, so they keep reading to the next slide. If you look at the left corner in your stories, you can see how many of your followers have seen that particular slide, which means that you can track how many people see slide 1, slide 2, slide 3, etc. Seeing how many people are opening your stories is important information because that can signal if they are interested in what you have to say. I usually have a story open rate of around 20%, and I'm happy with that. If you have a very low open rate, consider changing your profile picture.

The goal of slides 2-3 is to build desire and have my followers keep reading. I'm usually trying to connect to the benefits of using my product in these slides.

Slides 4-6 are all about getting my followers to act. Acting usually means sending a DM or visiting my website. Depending on what you sell, acting can mean a bunch of things. And as I said before, whenever you get a DM from someone, treat it seriously. The person is most likely interested in what you have to offer.

Talk about your offer in IG Live Video

This is a relatively new feature. It's a type of video streamed on the platform as it's being recorded, meaning you can broadcast your videos live to your followers. This is an excellent idea for businesses looking to build stronger relationships with their followers. The benefit of Instagram Live is it's more engaging than any other form of video. People can comment and ask questions in real-time, and you can answer and engage with them.

This way, you could easily make monthly updates by reading and replying to comments or by making videos in response to the comments. This is an excellent way to communicate with your target audience and allow them to connect with you on a more personal level. IG Live is also great for making announcements if you have important news to share with your followers. Here are some tips to help you make the most of IG Live:

- Be prepared to respond to real-time comments during your broadcast.
- Don't broadcast forever. Limit your broadcast to 30 minutes to keep people engaged and wanting more.
- Make sure you tell people that you'll be going live on Instagram in advance.

Going live is fairly simple, and it only takes a few clicks to start broadcasting. Once you start your broadcast, your followers will see your story in the "Live" top section of their feed. You can even set up multiple cameras to broadcast different angles. Let's take the example of the Instagrammer @adrian_rodriguez. He owns a fitness company that offers personalized plans to help people get into shape. Adrian regularly uses Instagram Live to broadcast his workouts in real-time, which his followers love!

Talk about your offer in your feed - the living room strategy

There's much talk about whether it's important to have an organized and nice-looking feed or not. In my opinion, as long as you haven't nailed everything else we have talked about in this book, a nice-looking feed is not magically going to get your followers to hand you money. In my experience, feed posts can contribute to sales, but stories are a much more effective sales tool. So is the feed not important? It is. When I think about the IG feed, I think about entering a living room. I have a little bit of everything in my living room; photos, arts, furniture, instruments, and books. In my opinion, the IG feed is kind of a living room. When new potential followers check out your feed, they usually skim the first 6-9 posts. If all you do is showcase your product and do promo, promo, and promo, what will they think? They might not want to follow you. On the other hand, if you have that living room vibe on your feed, it feels connected, and you are inviting them to follow you. I've had people coming to my feed and instantly reaching out for coaching because my feed connected with them.

Plan your feed posts in advance

An exercise I started with recently is to plan my feed posts in advance. The way I do it is simple and requires a simple pen and paper. I draw 12 squares, each representing a slot in my feed. I try to do two feed posts per week, which means I plan my feed six weeks in advance. What I try to accomplish with this planning exercise is a nice balance between all areas of my business and making sure I get that living room vibe in my feed.

Here's how the exercise looks:

IG plan

Benefits of self publishing Date:	**Engagement video** Date:	**Pic of me outside** Date:
FAQ Date:	**Book recommendation: Profit First** Date:	**Royalties feb** Date:
Video: Current trends on Amz Date:	**Testimonial from client** Date:	**Pic when I sit in the couch and read** Date:
Start up costs Date:	**Three tips for making money on Amazon** Date:	**Post about my lead magne** Date:

If you want to do this exercise yourself, think about how all these posts will fit in your overall business funnel. Remember, the goal is not just to post beautiful images. The goal is to connect with your followers on their heroes' journeys.

Ask for testimonials and feature People Who Use Your Product

One way to talk about your offer without talking about it is to use testimonials from previous customers. When I ask about testimonials, I send my customers six questions. Here are the six questions I use when I ask for testimonials about my coaching program.

1. What was your biggest concern before buying my coaching program?

2. What kind of result have you got from taking the program?

3. Can you mention one thing that was over your expectations?

4. Can you mention two more things you were happy with?

5. Would you recommend other people to buy this program? If so, why?

6. Is there something you want to change/add to the
   program?

Depending on what you sell, one way of keeping your
product relevant to your audience and keeping the marking
rule of seven going is by giving your followers insights into
the type of people who are using your product. This is a
popular strategy within the wellness industry. For example,
paying for big-name influencers to wear a piece of clothing.
Personally, I would not overspend on this strategy at the
beginning. As long as you have a deep interest in giving your
followers what they want and connecting with them, you
don't need to hire expensive influencers to market your
products.

Think in terms of campaigns, not posts

When you know the purpose of your IG account and where in
your business IG lives, it becomes clear that IG is just a tool
to grow your business. To make money and grow your
business, you need to sell something, and to sell something,
your best bet is to run som kind of campaign. There are tons
of different kinds of campaigns, including launch campaigns,
traffic campaigns, awareness campaigns, etc.

When I talk about campaigns here, I don't mean paid ads.
What I mean by a campaign is the collection of all your
efforts during a limited time to reach a specific goal. It's all
the posts, videos, reels, and stories you are doing during a
fixed period (3 days, seven days, or 30 days) to get your
followers to buy whatever you are selling.

Plan to the end

You can keep a few things in mind to increase the chances of running a successful campaign. The first thing is to plan to the end, which means mapping out all the posts, videos, reels, etc. you will do before you start. Then, all you need to do is execute your plan, which is much easier than winging it and posting whatever you feel like. The second thing to keep in mind to run a successful campaign is to set a goal of what you hope to accomplish. By planning and setting goals, you have something to measure and evaluate afterward, and it's easier to draw valuable lessons from your efforts.

Your campaign window

The most common campaign strategy is to focus all your efforts during a limited period. Of course, you have to decide which period works for you, but I recommend trying at least three to seven days and seeing what happens. During that limited time, you mobilize everything you got and do everything you can to get as many of your followers to buy your product, sign up for your course, join your webinar or visit your homepage as possible. During this particular time window, your goal is to get your followers to see your offer more than once, connect with them, and induce a bit of scarcity if they are not taking action.

When you plan your campaign, whether it's a 3-day, 7-day, or 30-day campaign, you can use this structure:

<u>Step 1: The big reveal</u>

Reveal to your followers that you will launch a product and talk about your product's benefits (not the features).

Step 2: The free taste

Give your followers a peek behind the curtains and give away a free taste.

Step 3: The last chance

Scarcity triggers action, so make sure to communicate when you close the doors. Then, give your followers a last chance to join.

This structure is just a broad framework. For example, if you are doing a 21-day launch, you might spend the first 4-5 days revealing your product, the next 7-10 days to give away a free taste, and the last few days to induce scarcity.

When my friend Marie launched a coaching program to her 600 followers, here is how she planned it:

Week 1

M: Reel - five things I want to create in 2022
T: Stories - Q&A - what do you want to create in 2022?
W: Feed post – Selfie
T: Multi slide feed post - 5 tips that helped me do X
F: Stories - yes/no questions to your Tribe

S: n/a
S: Stories: sharing other accounts

Week 2

M: Reel - try this if you want to accomplish X
T: Stories – entertaining
W: Feed post - share your favorite quote, ask your followers for theirs
T: Multi slide feed post - 5 myths about X

F: Stories - book recommendations
S: n/a
S: Stories: sharing the last time you learned something

Week 3

M: Reel - 8 days left to launch
T: Stories - share testimonials etc
W: Selfie post - share why you are doing this (your story)
T: Multi slide feed post - "the best way to do X."
F: Stories - Q&A "how would your life change if you accomplished X?"
S: Feed: Share something personal
S: Stories: 48hr to launch!

Week 4

M: Reel - 24 to launch
T: Stories - Open! Join now!
W: n/a
T: Multi slide feed post - "talk about how your product solves

a real problem."
F: Stories - Closing soon, more free tastes
S: Live video: Keep mentioning the benefits of your product
+ live Q & A
S: Stories: Last call!

Ways to Monetize

IG offers a multitude of ways to make money. The most common ones are selling your own product or service, affiliate marketing, or subscriptions. I know solo entrepreneurs and small businesses in all these fields, and from my experience, high ticket offers the most profitable products to sell on IG. That being said, you might find success with affiliate marketing, so it's always best to test what works for you. So let's look at how to monetize your IG account in different ways.

How to write a money-making bio

Your IG bio is very important and can be a determining factor if your followers end up buying from you, as well as for whether you get new followers or not. More than your photo, you have your username, 150 characters to describe yourself and/or your business, space for a URL link, and space for a series of highlights.

When it comes to the username, you should try to be as clear as possible. For example, I have the IG name @inkomstmedbocker (translated into English, it becomes @incomewithbooks). Pretty clear what my account is about, right? If the followers immediately get a feel for what your account is about just by reading your username, you have won a lot. Then you can use your profile picture and the 150 characters to connect to them even more deeply without wasting time explaining what your account is about.

As an example, this is how my bio looks:

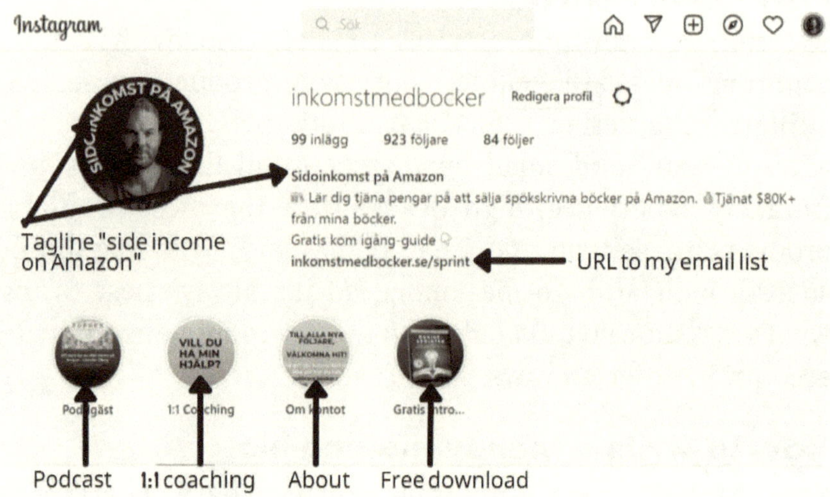

The purpose of my bio-text is to get more followers, but above all, it is to get traffic to my website with the hope of getting more email subscribers, which is in line with my business funnel.

Highlights in the bio

You can include highlights from stories in your bio. I see this a bit like a menu bar on a website. For example, I have an "about" highlight, a highlight about the coaching programs I sell, one about podcasts I've been to, and finally, a highlight to my lead magnet. I do not know if the highlights contribute to more followers and increased sales. Still, in any case, it gives you the chance to provide your followers with an even better picture of who you are or what your company is about, so I recommend you take advantage of that.

Selling low price products on IG

You can make money by selling physical products or digital downloads on IG. If you're an artist, you can offer your physical products (artwork, records, merchandise, etc.). If you run a small business, you can sell digital downloads of reports or eBooks. From my experience, mainly talking to authors, it's pretty damn hard to sell low-price items on IG. I know a few people with a ton of followers (25k+) who struggle to sell even a handful of units. I don't know why that is, but I would advise you not to only sell low-priced items on IG. If you run an e-commerce store, you can use IG as a traffic source and make money that way. That being said, companies such as Stella and Dot (jewelry), Scentsy (scented items), and Jamberry (nail decals) have made a fortune selling their products through IG, so everything is possible.

Affiliate Marketing on IG

If you have an already well-established following on IG, promoting affiliate products is one way to make money. I know a guy in the personal finance space. He made $12,000 in affiliate commissions in 2021 from around 10k followers. He finds his affiliate products on sites like Adrecord, and he's promoting investment bank accounts. Making money on affiliate commissions is not easy because you often need a large following, and you are most likely promoting the same affiliate products as many others IG accounts. In my opinion, if you are only promoting affiliate products, you are leaving a ton of money on the table. Big money on IG will come from selling your own product or service.

Premium Content Subscription

Some people sell access to their premium stories as a subscription service. This is similar to Patreon, in that subscribers pay a monthly fee to gain access to their content. To be successful, you need a large following and valuable content. I know a guy, also in the personal finance space, who shares all the stocks he buys/sells and shares his thoughts about the stock market. He started his premium stories in July 2021. He had 18k IG followers, and 100 people signed up the first month. He kept talking about his premium service every day (marketing rule of seven), and at the end of 2021, 550 people had signed up. He charges $10/month, so that's a $5,500/month IG income right there. I like to compare this type of income to the early stages of launching a podcast or YouTube channel. While you won't make much money at first, your audience will grow over time, and you can make exponentially more money. Think about if you have anything to package and sell like a subscription service.

Create Your Product or service

This is my favorite way of making money on IG! I have talked repeatedly about how important it is to know your followers, and when you do, you can create a product or service they will love. A typical product is to create some kind of course.

Sales tool: How to master your sales calls

When people schedule a call with you, they're taking time out of their day to see what you have to offer. So prepare ahead and make it worth their time. Lead the conversation. That way, you know what to say and how to tackle the questions you get. Here's how to do it.

Set the Agenda

Set the agenda. This will help keep your call on track. Do this by breaking the agenda up into three parts.

First, build connection and ask questions like "why did you reach out to me?", "what are the results you are looking for?", "why is that important to you?"

When you have a bit of background, and a better feel for why they wanted to jump on a sales call with you, keep digging to find out if they have tried to solve their "problem" in any other way before. Ask, "have you tried to [instert the result they want] before?" if they say yes, ask in what way and keep digging. If they say no, ask, "what do you think is your biggest challenge to reach [result]?".

Then, circle back to what you have heard and position your product as the solution to their problem (if it's a good fit!), and talk about the benefits of using your product. Ask if they want to buy your product/ book a session, and keep talking about the benefits they will experience for using your product. Finally, you can share details about how it works behind the scenes, arrange the payments and thank them for their time.

Final reflections about making money on IG

A couple of years ago, when I was completely new to online business, I watched a Youtube video about how important it is to have the right mindset to succeed in business. In that clip, I clearly remember that they said that your business is a mirror image of yourself. I never really understood what that meant back then, but now I do.

In a way, entrepreneurship is a bit like disguised self-development. It is difficult, or almost impossible, to build a successful business without working on yourself, your habits, fears, etc.

Imagine that you feel it's scary to start with video on IG, but you know that video connects much better than regular posts and that video is what will be required if you want to maximize your chances of making money. How do you go about starting with video? You work with your fears, and you take small steps forward until one day when you are confident of recording a video and posting it online. In this way, the development of your business is a direct mirror image of the way you are developing yourself.

You will face many uncomfortable things as soon as you start seeing IG as an income stream. It's easy to get carried away and drawn into what everyone else is doing, how well everyone else is editing their posts, and how many followers everyone else seems to have. To not be affected by what everyone else does, you need to work on yourself and learn how to care less about what people think and feel about you. Your work with yourself will spill over into your business, and you will notice how you constantly need to learn more about yourself to make money on IG.

Now, put yourselves out there and start treating IG like an income stream!

Connect with the author

There are plenty of Instagram books out there, so thank you for choosing this one and reading to the end!

I hope I have given you something worth your time, despite not being a native English writer.

What I hate after reading a book is the feeling that it's stuffed with bad and boring content that's easily found for free online If I gave you that, let me know in the reviews. But, on the other hand, If I gave you what you expected (or more), please tell me that in the reviews!

If you want to connect with me, learn all about Swedish Fika, and get my monthly marketing email Swedish Fika and Marketing Strategies, go to: christianoberg.com/strategies

And if you liked this book, check out my other book *Likes Don't Pay Bills*.

Regards,
Christian Oberg
christianoberg.com
IG: @inkomstmedbocker

www.ingramcontent.com/pod-product-compliance
Lightning Source LLC
Chambersburg PA
CBHW031804150726

47989CB00006B/2870